To Free the Sisters of Mary

Mattie McClane

Myrtle Hedge Press

Copyright © 2022
Myrtle Hedge Press, Kure Beach, North Carolina

ISBN 978-1-7329970-2-8
Library of Congress Control Number 2021949606

Design by Val Sherer, Personalized Publishing Services
Photo 26721991 © Claudio Giovanni Colombo | Dreamstime.com

"*The connections between and among women are the most feared, the most problematic, and the most potentially transforming force on the planet.*"

–Adrienne Rich

Preface

I was listening to Adrienne Rich's recorded poetry reading from the 1990s, and she referenced the "women's liberation movement." In 2021, the words seem antiquated, as if women have moved past the need to be freed. The truth is women now occupy space in most professions.

They are doctors and lawyers. They are elected to legislative halls and vote on important bills, affecting global policies. Yet, young girls are affronted with celebrity icons who are popularly compelled to bare their bodies, supporting the idea that women are still majorly objectified in in culture. Patriarchy still informs women's identities, making them unfree, unequal, and thus unsafe.

There is a continued need to liberate women from the accepted cultural norms that promote violence and often hidden forms of oppression. Women will not be free or safe anywhere in the world until the Catholic Church with its 1.3 billion worldwide members changes its views and allows women to be ordained as deacons and priests. Women do not have equal status in the Church, therefore culture.

The Catholic Church participates wittingly or unwittingly in widespread misogyny. In the past, feminist women have left the Catholic Church rather than insist it change its ideas. In more cynical moments, I think the Church hierarchy welcomes their departure; the headache is gone. Yet the Catholic Church cannot exist without the help of millions of ordinary women. Everyday Catholic women can demand change; and the world changes, when we free sisters of Mary.

Mattie McClane
December, 2021
Wilmington, North Carolina

To Free the Sisters
of Mary

I

The power is out
in New Orleans
from Hurricane Ida
a mighty river reverses
its course. Will young
men prophesy
and the old dream
of signs? It is a time
to proclaim
that the world
will be new
with its powerful CEOs
in coats
and opened shirts
the relaxed look
there are no
more obstacles

to fairness. They
have consumed
enough taken
mashed sweet potato
from the toddler's mouth.
The light is coming
for you, from a mountain
with three tents
you shall see it
a dazzling spectacle
and share a secret
that will be known
in time, when all
is known
the busy bodies
who broadcast
the news
will be struck

mute from tireless
forecasting
self-serving pundits
in search of the big job
in prime time.
How much
do they pay
for you to spout
the agreed upon script
in a country
that has grown
accustomed
to falsehoods?
What is it
your children
put on school forms
when ask what
you do for a living?

Mine is a fabricator
a storyteller
for corporations
for a member
of Congress
great professions
that are bought
and sold. Turn off
the big box
that noise maker
of mass communication
of the people
who would
not rewrite history
but yesterday's happenings
or that
of weeks ago
or months ago

when the eyes
still remember
and are not healed.

I recall a documentary
about China
when its government
would put
loudspeakers
at the top
of street poles,
indoctrinating
spreading
the party's news.
In our country,
we turn them on
in living rooms. The

host's lead voice
interviews others
all speculation
all guessing
all narratives
to affect
to manipulate
power standings
a second
Catholic president
beaten down
by daily criticism.
Have we so
quickly forgotten
who came before him?
We have not forgotten
but someone's profit
is ailing,

is falling
the chaos sells
when people
only want
to go for a walk
to fall in love
hum melodies
have birthday parties,
the loss
of private lives
to public strife.

I have watched
democracy diminished.
I have seen millionaires
become billionaires
while people survive
on donated food.

I will say
that it is over,
the great inequality.
In my imagination,
I hear you laugh
a chuckle
then a roar.
Who am I, you say
to declare
such a change
in fortune?
I am a witness
I am a poet
I am a proclaimer
like when
Lincoln announced
the slaves were free
through

the Emancipation
Proclamation or when
Luther tacked
his thesis to
the Church's door.
It needs
to be stated,
it needs to be said
before it happens.
The long term
design
the plan
that isn't mine
is put in motion
no one
really denies
that some
should not go hungry

while others invite
friends on space flights.

Please understand
that the only tool
I have is words. They
won't numb
you like vodka
but you will
want a shot
after you see
the truth
in them.
You will huddle
with cohorts
and wonder what
is to be done. You
will hide them, erase

them, knowing
somewhere
in your mind
in the history of silence
"that truth
crushed to earth
will rise again."
A man said that,
so maybe you will listen.

You learned of your power
when you took
the Massachusetts woman
down. You locked
her out, ignored her
didn't invite
or broadcast
her opinion

until her fans dropped
away and her money dried up.
It's an age-old tactic.
Just ignore
the outspoken woman,
put her
in your sound-proof cage
until she feels
she cannot breathe
charge her
with hysteria,
claim she is a radical
the worst ever
a heretic
a whore
maybe a Socialist
or a Communist, define
her as undependable

Name her Mary.
I will free
her sisters,
free the sisters
of Mary.

The levees hold
against deluge
there is much damage
some loss of life
the oil fields
are disrupted
scientists say the two
are linked. How
many hurricanes
will Louisiana endure?
How many

mildew-streaked
FEMA trailers
will house
the displaced
women with
six children
after years
have passed
and the big box
focuses on the
girls in tribal lands?
The oil money stains
the hearts
of lawmakers
soils the minds
of Gulf citizens fills
the coffers
of candidates

all in for the world's
warming.

The young
will have visions
the elderly's dreams
become crowded
with beloveds
the prolonged kisses
on bare skin
the snow
a frozen shower
slushy pearls
falling outside
a picture
window adds
to the sentiment
of a quiet place

in winter

to be in

on a day when

the private

was so real

it was unnoticeable

accessible

attainable

reserved

for investigative

journalists

living

for curiosity

and adventure.

Ideology

was present

and unmoving

Barry Goldwater types

with skinny ties
mostly shunned
loved by
the worst
of extremists.

You will surveil me
and not know where
my power comes from.

Her name was Julissa.
She was born
registered
as a welfare
baby reunited
to a known
abusive family.
She was seven years old

when found dead
beaten
a trauma
to the abdomen.
She was last
seen with a food voucher
waiting for a sandwich
at a vendor.
She crossed
a busiest city intersection
alone, everyone knew
she was alone
but did not interfere.
Her brother killed her
because she ate his snacks
for supper.

Name her

Mary, it is my greatest
hope to free the sisters
of Mary.

The time is here
when the weak prevail
they come out
of their hiding
their shelters
their backrooms
their caves
and stairwells
the lepers
with the affected limbs
are relocated
to an island
in paradise.
It has been said.

It has been written
Who am I
to doubt
the power
of language
of a higher will
aimed at
goodness
sweetness
and light?
It portends
the end
of hatred
of falsehood
of battles
of might
of hollow men
who torture

and kill
the vulnerable.

II

Write a poem about men
and some will rush
to the bookstore
or search
for it online.
They will want
to see if there
is flattery
any deserved glory
about obvious
heroics.
They want
to know
if the narrative
is about guns
about conquests
in exotic locales.

Write about women
and they expect
the same.
Women escape
notice
unless they
are in glossy
photographs
are young
or a toned 56
and can fit
into a leopard print
or are seen on
the arms
of sports figures.

Name her Mary. I want
to free the sisters of Mary.

The Catholic Church
is a brotherhood
a hierarchy
of robed men
who allow
women religious
to serve
to work
to labor
for parishes
while never letting
them set policy
or act as priests.
I suggest,
as one who loves

the Church,
that this is over. Lives
have been spent
fighting
the domination.
The woman
is considered
inferior
not by God
but by colleagues.
She is obedient
to tradition
and the biases
of old clergy.

Name her Mary, I am
called to free
the sisters of Mary.

Religion must
free its women
in cultures around
the world.
If in these, women
were equal
there would be
a sound
of freedom
so real
so joyous
so wonderful
so rapturous
so happy
that music
would play
bells would

tumble
and roll
sounding
in towers
until the moon
meets the morning sun.
Girls could settle
into community schools
there would
be no limits.

The storm moves
to Mississippi
up to New York.
The concern
is about heavy
rainfall.
Residents assess

the damage
to property
the fallen trees
the torn roofs.
Evacuees return home
anxious
and weary.
There are limitations
to words
to poetry
but the proclamation
is endless hope
is a promise
Christ's model
his example
from a mountaintop
where he called
for the Kingdom

It endures
and finds its way.

An open black book
with gold lettering
is set on a dictionary stand.
It contains
so many words
they signify
the potato peeler
the automobile
whirring machines
without emotion
every human sentiment
is felt most
when passionately
in love.
Once I put humiliation

into words
and am better
for it.

Great anger goes
into words
and there is no victory.
It is easy
to express.
It burns its way
onto paper
until all
is consumed
leaving nothing.
So be resolute
say the world
matters
is important

is worthwhile
even in
its current form
with troubles
and strife.
Say that after
the disappointment
of history people
will change
but they
will need
to read
four gospels
the social philosophers
the diaries
of part-time lunatics
and thinkers.
Whatever they read,

they will learn.

My words recognize
the price
the toll
the requirements
to go forward
in a time when
grace
leniency
mercy
seem over
and the law prevails
I remember the day
when I rushed
into the Sunday chapel
and knew.
I could see

the reversal.
The trials
would be real
the yoke
would be
placed
on shoulders
then bruising
then grooving
then sculpting
the flesh
the senses
of yesterday's holy
followers.

What I do today
will affect 20 years
from now

unworked legs
become soft;
shelved books
create stale minds.
Then there
are the read volumes
the Boston ad
and the ministry school.
It all comes back
perfectly
a messenger pigeon.
The present
catapults itself
into invisible hours
the birds
I see today
will have broken nests
straw gray

and dusty
with a bit
of a fisherman's string.
or clumps
of animal hair.
Time shows
me the past,
and I will know
the exact focus
of the future.

III

1.   Frances Perkins
FDR's labor secretary
is a footnote
on a page
that says she
actually wrote
The New Deal
an important
economic plan.
President Roosevelt
took credit
for her brainpower
for helping
the suffering
millions
in breadlines.
How many times

does the man
take the glory
the recognition
for a woman's work?
How many times
does she collude
with mistreatment
cast her lot
with glamorous
well- constructed
Yahoo page
celebrities
who would
shape their bodies
with a surgeon's
knife?

2.   Adrienne Rich
     knew the potential
     of poetry.
     Words are
     accountable.
     How beautifully
     you explain
     what is in every
     poet's mind before
     she/he/ they
     write the words
     on the screen
     The poetry frees
     cowardly impulses
     putting into
     sentences
     jarring witness.
     You still teach

You did not die
but have "verbal privilege"
your words ran
fast through
my mind
I imagine
that I discovered
you, your command
of language
at a fateful time.

3.   Margaret Fuller
Hawthorne's muse,
the model
for Prynne
became a shipwrecked mother
of letters
a journalist
a war correspondent

a Transcendentalist
who is mostly
forgotten
removed
from stories
of Emerson
of Thoreau
the intellectuals
who could
not understand
the desire
to educate women.

4. Dorothy Day,
    a bohemian youth
    later a convert
    who worked
    tirelessly
    for the poor, who

was vilified
for entering
the political realm
and called
the most radical
candidate
for sainthood,
a Communist,
and an anarchist.
She was made
a Servant of God
and left on
the Vatican's porch

IV

Holy Mary, pray for us.
Holy woman of God …
Holy woman of women

Woman … of Christ …
Woman … of divine grace …
Woman … most amiable …
Woman … most admirable …
Woman … of good counsel …
Woman … of our Creator …
Woman … of our Savior …

Woman … most prudent …
Woman … most venerable …
Woman … most renowned
Woman … most powerful …
Woman … most merciful …

Woman … most faithful …

Mirror of Justice …
Seat of Wisdom …
Cause of our joy …
Spiritual Vessel …
Vessel of Honor …
Singular Vessel
of Devotion …
Mystical Rose …
Tower of David …
Tower of Ivory …
House of Gold …
Ark of the Covenant …
Gate of Heaven …
Morning Star …
Health of the Sick …
Refuge of Sinners …

Comforter
of the Afflicted …
Help of Christians …

Woman … of Angels …
Woman … of Prophets …
Woman … of Apostles …
Woman … of Martyrs …
Woman … of Confessors …
Woman … Conceived
without Original Sin …
Woman … Assumed
into Heaven …
Woman … of the Most Holy Rosary …
Pray for us, O Holy Woman of God.

V

Finally, the open door
bright air
bricks fall
concrete exposes
broken
bent steel rods
that have kept her
so unheard.
She has been yelling
inside thick walls.
Now she steps out
amazed
at freedom
there is the unbelievable
the impossible
stacked straw
sweaty livestock

nature's mute feeling
inarticulate life
The outside knows her.
Her words
are faint at first
She reminds them
and they recall
the restraints, cut skin,
bruised bones
from trying to walk
on a straight path
She is through
the passage
her gait is steady
and shoes sound
one after another
She moves forward
without barricades

to be arriving
at anticipated places
the proclamation
the lifted voice
announces sings
about confinement's end

Painful fetters
of tradition
of old habits
are broken.
Let the woman
remember
what holds her
what keeps her
tied to salons
the all-color
discount

the French manicure
the dream
of baubles
of objects
of rooms
with the ultimate
tanning booth.
No, fill young minds
with equations
and musical
theories
for the piano
for symphonies
fill the young
with self-knowledge
with a passion
for unity.
Sit them

on wooden
stools
to study galaxies.
Let them count
the glittering stars
measure
the black holes
and make plans
to speak
to publish papers
on hurricanes
on the Earth
on climate change
let listeners
be of choice
who will hear
the sounds
in solar-powered

buildings
with open
windows
and welcoming
doors.

Atlantic disturbances
are reversing
wide rivers.
Harvard University
divests its endowments
from fossil
fuel companies
after alumni
protests.
The power goes out
in the sweltering
Southern cities

without AC.
Will young women
prophesy
while the old ones
dream dreams?
Perhaps they know
the sisters
are free, free
are the sisters of Mary.

About the Author

Mattie McClane is an American novelist, poet, and journalist. She is the second and youngest daughter born to James L. and Shirlie I. Myers in Moline, Illinois. Her father was a commercial artist and her mother worked as a secretary.

McClane's earliest education was in the Catholic schools. Her experience with their teachings deeply affected her. At a young age, she became aware of gender inequality. She credits her early religious instruction for making her think about "all kinds of truths and ethical matters."

McClane's parents divorced when she was eight years old. Her mother remarried attorney John G. Ames and the new couple moved to a house beside the Rock River. The river centrally figures in McClane's creative imagination. She describes her childhood as being "extraordinarily free and close to nature."

McClane moved to Colorado and married John Kaiser in 1979 in Aurora, just East of Denver.

They then moved to Bettendorf, Iowa, where they had three children. John worked as a chemist. Mattie became interested in politics, joining the local League of Women Voters. According to McClane, she spent her 20s "caring for young children and working for good government."

She graduated from Augustana College with a B.A. degree in the Humanities. She began writing a political column for Quad-Cities Online and Small Newspaper Group, based in Illinois.

Her family moved to Louisville, Kentucky where she continued with her journalism and then earned an M.A. in English from the University of Louisville. Critically acclaimed author Sena Jeter Naslund directed her first creative thesis, "Unbuttoning Light and Other Stories," which was later published in a collection.

She was accepted to the University of North Carolina at Wilmington's M.F.A. in Creative Writing Program, where she wrote the short novel *Night Ship*, working under the tutelage of Pulitzer Prize winning author Alison Lurie. McClane studied with Dennis Sampson in poetry also. She graduated in 1999.

She would write a column for the *High Point Enterprise* in North Carolina. She would later write for the *News and Observer*. McClane has regularly published commentary for over 25 years.

Mattie McClane is the author of *Night Ship: A Voyage of Discovery* (2003, 2017), *River Hymn: Essays Evangelical and Political* (2004), *Wen Wilson* (2009, 2022), *Unbuttoning Light: The Collected Short Stories of Mattie McClane* (2012), *Now Time* (2013), *Stations of the Cross* (2016), *The Mother Word, An Exploration of the Visual* (2017), *Simeon's Canticle* (2018), *The Magnificent Light of Morning* (2021), *To Free the Sisters of Mary* (2022).

She lives in North Carolina.